GOVERNMENT ANARCHY

GOVERNMENT ANARCHY

BRITT STORKSON

To order additional copies of this book, contact:
Xlibris
1-888-795-4274
www.Xlibris.com
Orders@Xlibris.com
792380

CONTENTS

Foreword

Government, even in its best state, is but a necessary evil; in its worst state, an intolerable one. – Thomas Paine.

Preface

Visionary and former President Ronald Reagan once said that "Government that is big enough to give us everything we want can also take from us everything we have". Starting around the time of Franklin Roosevelt in the 1930's we began expecting government to give us everything we wanted. We now are approaching the latter part of this proclamation where government is taking most everything that we have. This is the legacy of unlimited government.

We have piled up more government debt than any other country in history. We even borrow money and then give it to various nations around the world under the moniker of "foreign aid" which is not much more than corporate welfare. Most of this money ends up in the pockets of the ruling classes of these various countries with very little going to improve the lives of the average citizens our government claims to be helping.

Our government is like the irresponsible college student who takes out student loans to finance trips to Europe and a lavish party lifestyle and ends up with a degree in art history. This student is not only unemployable but has all of this debt and no way to pay it back. Rush, Lars and Hannity maintain that our children will repay that debt. Wrong. They are simply not going to pay it. The debt is so huge they could not pay it back even if they wanted to.

Our economy is so fragile due to this unrestrained borrowing and spending we could face a major economic recession or depression condition if the Chinese (or other major players) simply refused to buy any more of our debt. They could conquer us without firing a shot.

China has already begun "repossessing" rail and shipping port facilities they built in Kenya (Africa) and other places by extending "easy credit" to these countries to pay for these projects and then taking the facilities for their own use when the countries could not pay them back.

The strategy is obvious: Build infrastructure such as rail, road and port terminals for local politicians looking for an easy "fix" for their economic problems. Get the irresponsible leaders to put up their countries' resources as collateral. Then wait a few years for the countries to get behind in their payments and then foreclose by taking the infrastructure for their own use. Sure sounds like what's happening in this country as well without the foreclosures…Yet.

And what about all of these projects providing jobs for the locals? Most of the good jobs go to the Chinese nationals and the locals get jobs, as one of the locals put it, "moving rocks".

Government borrowing has become so extreme and uncontrolled we have scenarios like the Kingdome in Seattle, Washington which was used for a time to house the Seattle football and baseball teams. The taxpayers finally paid off the loans to build it *14 years* after it had been torn down to make room for another stadium. The building was gone but the debt incurred to build the structure remained long after structure was gone.

Those in government have come to expect double-digit percentage increases in their budgets every year. Even "flatlining" by giving government agencies the same amount they received the prior year adjusted for inflation is often not good enough. Along with this would come rioting and other domestic turmoil with thousands protesting "austerity" measures.

All of this will end not because those in government will "wake up" and realize the error of their ways and change course. This will end when our government "leaders" cannot "buy off" anybody anymore with your tax dollars. When that happens they will simply strap on their golden parachutes and bail out.

In this treatise often refer to Rush, Lars and Hannity...Meaning Rush Limbaugh, Lars Larson and Sean Hannity. They are contemporary "conservative" radio talk show hosts preaching the doctrine of constitutional government.

They give us a lot to like…Us being those who champion freedom, liberty, and justice which is limited government. We can be very thankful to have them on the airwaves and they deserve our support. But there is a caveat: While unlike the mainstream media they do not lie to us they sometimes fail to report what should be significant news or don't tell us the entire story when they do report something.

Also do you notice how Rush, Lars and Hannity pretty much preach the same thing? It's like there's a common narrative or a template in that they almost always have the same "take" on a wide variety of subjects. Of course some things are indisputable but the fact that there is such consistent uniformity suggests that they are not independent thinkers.

These are my observations written in first-person narrative. These are general statements and there are exceptions. References or footnotes are omitted for brevity and readability. Most can be easily corroborated with some internet research. I have elected to focus on general concepts and not specific issues but will include current events from time to time as illustrations. "Current events" can change subsequent to this writing so parts of this work may not be up-to-date.

Chapter 1

Government Anarchy

First, the title: Government Anarchy. Anarchy is defined as: Absence of government and absolute freedom of the individual, regarded as a political ideal. Why the juxtaposition? Because that's what we have for government right now. We have government in place of course but also have a ruling class that gets and does pretty much whatever they want using campaign contributions to buy off our government "leaders".

This is not some large-scale conspiracy coordinated by a small group of power brokers residing in some bunker somewhere. This is simply what unlimited government is or becomes.

What's the difference between the mobster who tells a businessman that he needs to have a certain amount of money every month "or something bad will happen" and a government that demands a certain amount of money on a regular basis? Not much.

What's the difference between the government we have now and a third world nation where government officials demand bribes (known in U.S. as campaign contributions) from people to deliver tax dollars to them (also known as government programs) or make sure nothing bad happens to them (also known as "protection")? Not much.

Most of what federal, state and local governments spend money on now is driven by the campaign contribution, not by the desire to implement good public policy. Government has become a wealth re-distribution machine using the force of government with much of what the working class earns going to the very wealthy ruling class as well as the dependent class.

They do this often by enacting a myriad of laws but often not following or uniformly enforcing the laws they make. With the campaign contribution as the ruling force laws often get selectively enforced based on who gets how much from which campaign contributor.

While we're supposed to be a classless society we do have classes. I would classify our nation at this time as having three (3) distinct classes.

1. The working class: Those who produce goods and services that someone else is willing to pay for and they pay, as a percentage of or relative to what they earn (most often referred to as "tax burden") most of the taxes.
2. The ruling class. The 1% of the population who owns most everything including the politicians and who rule over us via force conferred by government and/or by possessing great wealth to buy those in government to do their bidding.
    While the ruling class is useful for providing investment capital which produces jobs for the working class they pay (relative to what they earn, not total dollars) very little in the way of taxes.
3. The dependent class. Those who are dependent on others and pay in taxes, as a percentage of what they get, more than the ruling class but less than the working class because they don't have that much to take.

First let's go over some really basic economics principles. Wealth is created by people who work doing or producing something that someone is willing to pay for either with money and/or barter. A food server works at a small restaurant serving tables and is paid an amount agreed upon by him or her and their employer. Both parties must agree to these terms or the server will not get paid or the service will not be delivered. The server can quit and go work somewhere else or the employer will refuse to pay the amount expected by the server and either goes without their services or finds someone else who will work the employer needs done for less money.

So wealth is created almost exclusively by the working class because they deliver a product or service that someone values enough to pay for. The employer may profit from the employee by charging the customer more than he pays the employee and keeps the difference in that a business is simply "selling" the employees' services or products made by these employees. There is nothing legally, ethically or morally wrong with that.

Consumers do the same thing. The consumer evaluates product offerings based on their needs and/or wants relative to the price demanded by the seller. The consumer is free to offer the seller a lower price but both parties must agree on the price and terms of sale or the transaction doesn't happen.

This has been going on since the beginning of time the world over in regardless of whatever government that is in place. This is called "commerce" and this happens even the most "hard-line" socialist countries. If the government tries to control or otherwise interfere with this commerce black markets soon spring up to service the demand. If there's a need or want for any product or service it isn't long before one or more businesses open up to profit by providing what the masses want or need. If you don't believe that just look at what happened with the marijuana business recently.

However the ruling class, using the force of government they have "bought into" via campaign contributions, has established a type of "Reverse Robin Hood". Instead of taking money from the rich and giving it to the poor government takes money from the working class and give is to the ruling and dependent classes. Some of the money does go back to the working class as well but they give to government far more than they gain or "get back". This is what happens when we have unlimited government and the remainder of this book will illustrate just how that is implemented.

Chapter 2

We have the best politicians money can buy

Money is first and foremost in American Politics right now. One can get virtually anything from government nowadays if one gives enough money to enough politicians. "Anything" includes money, protection (usually "get out of jail free" schemes that allow the campaign contributor to get away with doing something the average person would serve jail time for) as well as property that is "sold" to the campaign contributor in which the taxpayer picks up about 80% of the cost. All it takes is a few strategically placed campaign contributions usually routed through one or more lobbyists.

Rush, Lars and Hannity want us to believe that big business interests have the politicians "quaking in their boots" because of their power to tax and regulate. However just the opposite is true. It's the politicians who are "quaking in their boots" because they're hooked on campaign contributions just like a heroin addict is hooked on heroin.

The campaign contributor/politician relationship can be compared to the pathogen inside of a termite that will eat the termite if the termite doesn't eat enough of your house with the politician being the termite and the campaign contributor being the pathogen. Being greedy the campaign contributor demands more and more to eat while the politician, once "infected" with this pathogen, (and almost all are) has no choice but to deliver by eating you out of house and home to satisfy the campaign contributor.

And what about your house that they are eating? A little bit of termite damage won't be noticed nor will it compromise your house to any great degree. However given enough of this non-stop eating of your house and you won't have a place to live. And that's where we're heading as a nation. Does the politician purposely set out to eat you out of house and home? No. But the politician has a "higher order" (campaign contributors) that supersedes your need for a place to live. The politician doesn't care about you. He/she cares about getting campaign contributions.

Campaign finance laws are a joke. There are many ways to give money to politicians both openly and secretly…and all of the legal (or not illegal). One example: It is illegal for monopoly utilities to give money directly to politicians. Note the word "directly" here. But it is not illegal to give money to the politicians indirectly.

How do they do that? One way is to give money to trade organizations who then gives the money to the politicians. That is not illegal. It should be but it isn't. Most of us (and the IRS) would call this "money laundering" but it comes as no surprise that the politicians have legally re-defined money laundering and bribery when it comes to campaign contributions.

This "end run" also makes the money harder to track and there is no limit to how much money (including tax money) that can be spent on lawyers to stall or stop an inquiry. This also makes the campaign contribution tax deductible as a business expense.

Any politician can accept campaign contributions with only a few simple rules to follow to "keep it legal". And guess who enforces the campaign finance laws: The politicians who wrote them. The few that are prosecuted for campaign law violations are the stupid ones who didn't follow the rules that allow this money laundering/bribery to take place. And the ruling class doesn't mind purging the stupid from their ranks.

Even judges and county prosecutors can accept campaign contributions. Don't think for a second that doesn't impact the outcome of court cases or who gets charged for what crimes. It's obvious from the outcomes of various court cases across the country campaign contributions going to judges clearly do give the advantage to the campaign contributor.

Also politicians can still take campaign contributions if they are running unopposed or not running for re-election. Former U.S. Senator from Indiana Evan Bayh made about $13 million by continuing to take campaign contributions up until the end of his term and then converting the money to his personal use immediately after he left the Senate.

Ever wonder why outfits like Planned Parenthood, a private organization, keep getting taxpayer money year after year? It's mostly because part of our tax money given to them is "fed back" to politicians to make sure the money keeps flowing. Not because the politicians ideologically believe in abortion and euthanasia per se. It's because they can count on Planned Parenthood (and a lot of others) to feed some of the money they get back into their campaigns which ultimately ends up and benefitting them personally.

In fact the politicians even structure "their prices" based on how much money the organizations get from the taxpayers and expect a certain amount of "feedback funds". The "feedback" rule is roughly 20%. Meaning that if the taxpayers give a private organization $1 million then the politician(s) can expect somewhere on the order of $200,000.00 back in campaign contributions.

On top of that even foreigners and nations hostile to U.S. interests and national security can give campaign contributions…Usually "laundered" through one of many lobbyists that inhabit Washington D.C. and every state capitol in the country.

And what about the $25.00 campaign contribution making a difference in government like we're repeatedly told by the politicians? Think for a moment: Who gets their phone calls and e-mails answered by something other than a robocall or a "canned" message? The working class $25.00 contributor or the ruling class $25,000.00 contributor?

The problem is not money in politics. The problem is lack of full disclosure. Campaign finance reports produced for public consumption are not the same as the reports that go to the IRS. It's nothing more than keeping two sets of books which the politicians have legally re-defined as well.

I pointed this out to Lars Larson and asked him why we didn't get the same reports that the IRS gets when it comes to campaign contributions. He said because it "was private". Maybe he should ask former presidential candidate Mitt Romney about IRS privacy when he was accused by Senator Harry Reid of not paying taxes for 10 years. However I did not ask that the entire tax returns be produced. I simply asked for only the reports that go to the IRS detailing campaign finance transactions and Lars knew that.

Campaign contributions not only work to advance whatever the contributor wants it also buys the politicians' silence by motivating the politician to not oppose bad legislation. One way this happens is by use of the discharge petition. A discharge petition is a document the politicians sign to move a particular bill out of committee and on to the floor (of the house of representatives or senate) for a vote.

If the bill does not get out of committee it does not get a vote on the floor and it doesn't happen. So for every bill a discharge petition is circulated and the names on the discharge petition are secret. So congressman Blowhard can tell his constituents that he supports reducing the cost of health care but then refuse to sign the discharge petitions relating to bills that would reduce health care costs. That way the congressman has the best of both worlds: He gets to keep health care costs high to benefit his health care campaign contributors yet look like a "champion" working to lower health care costs to the voters.

Selling pardons at the end of a politicians' term has almost become routine. The politician has nothing to lose in the process. That is, nothing to lose except his/her reputation and "good name" which they probably never had to begin with. Nor did they care about that either. But that's what we get with unlimited government.

Chapter 3

We have one-party rule. It's called the MONEY party

Rush, Lars and Hannity want us to believe that there are sharp ideological differences separating the Democrat and Republican parties. Republican = good, Democrat = bad. Conservative = good, liberal = bad. In reality there is little difference between the political parties. Both are joined at the pocketbook of campaign contributions.

Typically the Democrats give our money to social welfare programs and the Republicans give our money to corporate welfare programs. Liberals, while claiming to be so compassionate, rarely spend their own money to help those in need. One way to quickly end illegal immigration is to enact a sponsor program where anybody who employed an illegal alien would be responsible for their support and personally liable for any crimes they commit. Instead the "little people" (working class taxpayers) in large part end up paying the bills and being victimized by their crimes.

But the problem is not being conservative or liberal. The problem is unlimited government. The British have realized the problems with unlimited governments by voting to cut ties with one of them: The European Union (EU). Not only did they have their own government to support with their tax dollars and regulate them with their bureaucrats but they had the European Union too. I wish them well in their efforts to exit the EU but once governments become unlimited it is very difficult to reduce or remove them. Often major change in government sparks a revolution where many lives are lost.

I would agree that there are a few fringe issues that differentiate the Democratic and Republican parties but overall the campaign contributors own the politicians and party affiliation, other than a path to public office is a non-issue.

This is easy to prove. Why do campaign contributors often give to both parties? It's because no matter which way the election goes they win. That's one reason why there is much resistance to more than two political parties: More impactful political parties means there are more politicians that need to be "bought off" costing the campaign contributors more money to get what they want.

The actual differences are not ideological but economic and elitist. Similarly the issue of human slavery in this country was not ideological but also economic and elitist. To Rush, Lars and Hannity the liberal is sort of a straw dog "villain" because the liberal ceases to exist when you take away other people's money (taxes). Contrary to what Rush says all of the time the Democrats do not want to create a "social utopia" with everybody being equal. They, along with everybody else in or "bought into" government operates the same way.

They are greedy and always seeking to increase their wealth. Since most of the wealth is created by the working class it's like the famous quote from the bank robber Willie Horton. When asked why he robbed banks he replied "because that's where all of the money is".

While the ruling class employs the working class to increase their wealth which is a moral and legitimate endeavor they also tax the working class to benefit the ruling class using the force of government which is an immoral and illegitimate endeavor. They are spending money to make more money and if that requires giving money to the politicians then that's what happens.

All people operate as capitalists buying at the lowest price they can get and selling at the highest price they can get in order to retain for themselves as much as they can. And there's nothing wrong with self-interest achieved honestly and ethically. Even the most oppressive governments have black markets that are purely capitalistic.

The problem comes when those who are in power use that power of government to funnel tax money to themselves via campaign contributions. Most of this is done in secret and in very indirect and discreet ways. But it is done all of the time.

These people are all about MONEY and being greedy they don't care who gets hurt in the process. Wealth has to come from somewhere and most of wealth is generated by the working class. But much of this wealth goes to the ruling class via government confiscation. If you get hurt in the process by higher taxes or oppressive regulation, well, that's just too bad. There is a "higher order" here. The campaign contributor is KING.

Again this is not a huge conspiracy with some powerful person or group "pulling the levers" somewhere. That's just what unlimited government is or becomes. Our founding fathers were keenly aware of the problems with unlimited government and that's why most of our U.S. Constitution deals with limiting government. "Congress shall make no law…" is repeated over and over again and for good reason.

Chapter 4

The worst swindlers and con artists aren't in jail. They're in Government

It's getting hard to tell the government scams from all the other scams out there.

Lars Larson has called Social Security the world's biggest Ponzi scheme and that's exactly what it is. Social Security is just another tax. There are all sorts of laws that force you pay into Social security but nothing in the law that says you can get anything back. There is no "lockbox", no account somewhere with your name on it. At least two U.S. Supreme court cases have affirmed that. At least with a private retirement your wealth is passed on to heirs but when you give the money to the government it's gone forever.

Regarding the "eeeeevil" environmentalists Rush, Lars and Hannity constantly reference as the source of most of our problems: Just who are they? Give us some names. Please explain how a few tree-huggers who live in the middle of nowhere and eat only bugs and berries are impacting our government. Where do these "back to nature" types get the money to hire teams of lawyers to advance their environmentalist agenda?

The fact is that the tree-huggers aren't doing much more than hugging trees. The environmentalist agenda is being advanced by the ruling class. I can cite many examples to illustrate this but I'll use the reduction of logging activity. There's no rational reason to "lock up" the forests by not logging them. But there are economic advantages for certain people to reduce lumber production. It's economics 101: Scarcity raises prices. Limiting the supply increases the price of almost everything.

Of course some of consequences of these actions are jobs lost in the logging and forest industries and increased forest fire activity of all of the dead and dry trees waiting for a spark to flare up. Things like this are not unintended consequences as Rush keeps telling us. The timber industry and the politicians know and understand that these policies have those consequences *but they don't care.* Campaign contributions trump the public interest and safety every time.

Even though this is factually indisputable how often do you hear Rush, Lars and Hannity talking about the big business interests that are using government via the campaign contribution to establish a de-facto monopoly to increase their wealth? Once I heard a forest management consultant being interviewed by Lars Larson say pretty much the same thing but Lars just ignored that point.

I can cite thousands of examples of this this phenomenon but let's take one example of air bags required to be installed in cars. Why don't we eliminate the requirements and let auto insurance companies offer discounts if there is an airbag in the car? Probably because air bags in cars do not significantly reduce auto crash deaths and injuries enough to have an impact on insurance costs.

But *required* air bags benefit the carmakers in other ways:

- There is no limit what the car companies can charge for these government-mandated devices.
- While making the car more expensive it also makes the car less reliable and more expensive to repair which the carmakers can blame on government.
- All of the "regulatory hurdles" cost staff time and money and expense discourages competitive "start-ups" who always seem

to make a better product at a lower cost and like most start-ups typically have limited funds.

- Of course there is nothing in the law that says these fees cannot be reduced or waived for certain people or organizations... Again depending on the size and scope of their campaign contributions.

I could write volumes detailing the many ways government swindles us out of our money and property. One way is to take advantage of the average persons' ignorance of the law. One day I went to work and came back to find power lines strung across my property. I called up the power company (Wasco Electric Cooperative based in The Dalles, Oregon) and asked the manager why they put power lines across my property without an easement or permission of any kind. He started giving me the "song and dance" of "we're the power company and we do whatever we want." Until I told him I was going to call my lawyer.

When he heard the word "lawyer" he quickly backtracked and offered to write a letter promising to remove the power lines whenever I wanted them moved. There were no conditions or timelines in this letter. Trying to be a "nice guy" and wanting to give people the benefit of the doubt I accepted the offer and he wrote a letter promising to move the power lines at any time if I wanted them moved some time in the future.

Eleven years later I decided to build a garage where the power lines were and called up the manager at the time. The manager refused to move the lines. I went to a lawyer with this letter (the promise from Wasco Electric to move the power lines) and found out that there's this law called Adverse Possession. Briefly it means if someone builds something on your property and you don't sue them within a certain period of time. This time varies from state to state...in Oregon it's currently 10 years. And written promises don't count when it comes to Adverse Possession claims.

The lawyers' research cost me $1200.00 so trying to be a "nice guy" cost me $1200.00. Here it's *not* what's in the law...not what's in the law that's significant. I learned that there is no law requiring the power company to have an easement or other permission to put power lines on your property. There should be but there isn't. Obtaining an easement and recording it at the county is a good practice and the right and ethical thing to do but one cannot enforce ethics in a court of law. I appealed to our state representative regarding this matter and he basically told me to "pound sand" because he's getting our (ratepayer) money from this power company.

Another way government swindles you out of your property is to regulate it to the point that it cannot be developed and therefore loses much of its value. But you still have to pay the taxes on it. The fifth Amendment to the U.S. constitution that states that private property shall not be taken for public use without just compensation. However the courts have held that regulating your property to the point of it losing most of its value does not constitute a "taking".

The government can, and at times should, take private property for public use and there is a legitimate way to do that. It's called "condemnation". When government "condemns" your property it buys it. That part is not disputed. The only part that is debated is the price. In the case of real property the price is usually determined by averaging three independent appraisals which gives the "seller" a reasonable assurance of getting a fair price. But often governments use regulation to take private property because it's cheaper and easier to hide from the public because it might make the politicians look bad and make it tougher to get re-elected.

We have a Political "dynasty" in large part because of the huge sums of money it takes to get elected to public office nowadays. Incumbency provides a great advantage in that incumbent politicians get re-elected about 96% of the time. It's very difficult to compete with someone who gives away money. I had a government worker one time tell me that it must be election time because there's all sorts of money available for government programs during the re-election time span.

While incumbent politicians like to look like they are available to the public most of the time the only people they interact with are the lobbyists. Often the politicians will issue a press release saying something like "I was in your town on this date meeting with my constituents" when nobody can remember hearing about this or that appearance. That's because the politician was not interested in meeting with the public so they tell the public they were in their town after the fact. You and I would not have friends like that. Why do we tolerate politicians like that? But that's what we get with unlimited government.

Chapter 5

The power to tax is the power to destroy

The power to tax is the power to destroy. This quotation comes from the words of DANIEL WEBSTER and those of JOHN MARSHALL in the Supreme Court case, McCulloch v. Maryland. Webster, in arguing the case, said: "An unlimited power to tax involves, necessarily, a power to destroy," 17 U.S. 327 (1819).

Why not enact a flat tax on everybody with no re-defining of income? It would be cheap and easy enforce and fair because everybody would bear the same tax burden equally. And that's exactly why we *don't* have a flat tax.

Taxation is nothing more than taking money or property by force. There is nothing in the law that requires that you get anything back. Once you give money to the government it's gone forever. Most of the time when a bond or levy is passed there is no guarantee that the money even goes there. Nor is there any penalty if the money is not spent on what was promised.

We don't even have government budgets anymore by the classic definition. We have "Omnibus spending bills" which are nothing more than huge chunks of cash that can be spent on anything and everything. In the not-too-distant past if a public school for example needed a new school bus the amount needed was determined by an open bidding process and that amount was submitted in a budget to be debated and accepted or rejected by an elected board of directors.

Now pretty much all money going to government is regarded as a blank check to be distributed as our politicians determine and usually to "pay off" campaign contributors. That's one reason we have "government grants" doled out by unelected bureaucrats who serve as cover for the politicians so if a good thing happens as a result it's the politician who gets the credit. If a bad thing happens then the unelected bureaucrat gets the blame even though he/she is just doing what the politician told him/her to do.

The politicians have many ways to extract money from us. They have been doing this for a long time and they are very good at it. Rulers have been imposing and exempting people from taxes almost since the beginnings of civilization. It's just what unlimited government does.

In the Bible the children of Israel demanded a king (unlimited government) and went from a 10% temple "tax" to oppressive tax rates just a few years after the king was installed. The tax burden increased so rapidly that 1 Samuel 17:25 tells us that King Saul offered highly desirable tax exemptions ("tax breaks") for anyone and their family who would take on the Philistine champion Goliath.

1 Samuel 8:10-18 tells us: 10) Samuel told all the words of the Lord to the people who were asking him for a king. 11) He said, "This is what the king who will reign over you will claim as his rights: He will take your sons and make them serve with his chariots and horses, and they will run in front of his chariots. 12) Some he will assign to be commanders of thousands and commanders of fifties, and others to plow his ground and reap his harvest, and still others to make weapons of war and equipment for his chariots. 13) He will take your daughters to be perfumers and cooks and bakers. 14) He will take the best of your fields and vineyards and olive groves and give them to his attendants. 15) He will take a tenth of your grain and of your vintage and give it to his officials and attendants. 16) Your male and female servants and the best of your cattle and donkeys he will take for his own use. 17) He will take a tenth of your flocks, and you yourselves will become his slaves.

18) When that day comes, you will cry out for relief from the king you have chosen, but the Lord will not answer you in that day."

This all came to pass exactly as Samuel had predicted. Notice verses 14 and 16 where it says "...He (the king/government) will take the best of your fields and...the best of your cattle and donkeys...". Taxes and lawyers almost always get paid first. When it comes to unlimited government basically nothing has changed over the last 3,000 + years.

Taxation is rarely uniformly applied or enforced as some people always end up paying more than others not relative to their ability to pay. Rush often cites how much the rich pay in taxes and, to them, that's a problem. But he always deals in total dollars. He downplays Warren Buffet's statement that his secretary pays more in taxes than he (a billionaire) does.

While it's true that the ruling class pays a lot in total dollars it's a token amount relative to what they make. Warren Buffet's secretary may pay less tax in total dollars but as a percentage of what she makes – what we would call the tax burden - she pays much more.

This underscores the great income disparity we now have in this country. But income disparity in itself isn't a problem. There's no problem with one growing wealthy by buying, selling and trading in the free market. The problem is how the wealthy obtain their wealth. About half of Elon Musks' (Tesla) personal fortune comes from the taxpayers. Instead of self-made millionaires we have government-made or taxpayer-made millionaires. This to go along with legitimate, profitable businesses they often own.

Taxation has become like merchandising where the "official" or "published" tax rate is not the rate that everybody pays. The "top marginal rate" is meaningless because "Discounts" are sold to the "best customers" meaning campaign contributors. The "top marginal rate" is simply a benchmark before all of the "discounts" (if any) are figured in. If you have a 70% top marginal rate and you have "discounts" worth 70% then you pay nothing. Or even get money back in some cases.

Taxation anymore is not solely to fund the government. Taxation is also used to reward the campaign contributors with tax breaks and punish those who don't "pony up" what the politicians demand in the way of campaign contributions. Those who don't "pony up" include most of us in the working class.

The tax system we have is ideal…For the ruling class as well as the government. The objectives are:

- Collect as much money as possible.
- Since it costs money to collect this money keep the collection costs as low as possible.
- Make it possible for people to pay reduced tax rates in exchange for campaign contributions.
- Provide refunds so people will think they are actually getting something back via the good graces of government.

One could not dream up a better tax system that delivers on the above objectives. While most of us dread "tax season" not just for the cost but for all of the time and stress it involves the IRS is the friend of the ruling class because they make it possible to for the ruling class to pay next to nothing in taxes relative to what they make. Plus this has spawned a huge industry just to deal with the task of paying your income taxes. The H and R Blocks, tax attorneys, accounts…All of them profit from the tax system we have.

When filing your taxes if you make a mistake in the governments' favor…Too bad. If you make even one mistake in your favor there's penalties and interest. And being very complex it's easy to make a mistake. That's by design. The tax code is also deliberately vague so the government can make up the rules as they go along. Most of the tax code is written not to impose taxes but to exempt certain people from paying them.

A few years ago I filed my state and federal taxes and somehow my unemployment earnings statement didn't make it into file when it was sent to the taxing authorities. About 6 months later I got this notice informing me that I owed additional taxes, interest and penalties for not reporting this income. Sure it takes some time to process the tax returns but 6 months? It's no accident that there is no statute of limitations on tax collections so the government can come after you for taxes years after you honestly thought you had paid what you owed.

Many are surprised to learn that the federal government did not tax their citizens during roughly the first half of our existence as a nation. From about 1787 to 1913 when the 16th amendment to the constitution was passed enacting an income tax. Prior to 1913 the government raised revenue primarily through "sin" taxes (mostly liquor) and tariffs. "Direct" taxes were not permitted. Our founding fathers well understood the evils of unlimited government and this is one of the ways they limited government.

Many wars have been fought over taxation. In 1 Kings 12:8-10 the Bible tells us about Solomon's son Rehoboam who was approached by the people to advocate reducing the heavy tax burden that his father Solomon had imposed upon them. Reheboam would not consider "tax relief" and that sparked a bloody civil war which ended up dividing the kingdom.

Our country – The United States - is the product of a tax protest. Recently the French reached a tipping point with a carbon tax triggering rioting by tax protesters in in Paris. There is a limit to everything and there is a limit to how much the ruling class can take from the working class before they revolt. And unlimited government is often what causes revolutions.

Chapter 6

The Golden Rule: He who has the gold makes the rules

We are supposed to be a nation of laws. But we have become a nation of "rules". What's the difference between a law and a rule? A law is introduced into the legislative body, debated and passed by a majority vote of the elected legislators. A "rule" (such as an administrative rule) has no such origin. A rule originates with some government bureaucrat and has the force of law because one must sue in a court of law to modify or repeal this rule.

The reason for this is that the politicians can impose their will on the people without having to answer for it on election day. They wring their hands and claim that some nameless, faceless, unelected bureaucrat did this – not them – and claim that they can't do anything about it.

That's simply not true because the politicians are the ones who hire and fire the bureaucrats. If, in the unlikely event that the bureaucrat doesn't do what the politician wants him to do that bureaucrat will most likely find himself/herself looking for another job. While this is factually indisputable how often do you hear Rush, Lars or Hannity talk about this?

It wouldn't be so bad if those with the "Gold" used "their Gold" to do this but most of the time that isn't the case. They use our "Gold" to get even more of "our Gold". How does this happen? It all goes back to campaign contributions. Our "gold" is taken from us in the form of taxation and part of the "gold" is fed back to the politicians to maintain this "gravy train".

When my wife, a Canadian, prepared to enter the country we retained an immigration lawyer to advise us. She demanded a $700 retainer and shortly thereafter "dumped us" saying she was too busy. No refunds. No apologies for taking our money and leaving us "in the lurch" as well as costing us more money in other areas.

While this was very unethical it is not illegal and it doesn't do any good to complain to the state Bar association. They exist to protect bad lawyers, not discipline them. Why do lawyers do this sort of thing to their clients? Because they can. They have the gold and they make the rules.

In Oregon if you're a farmer you get legal fees if you prevail in a court action. Nobody else does. Why do farmers get awarded legal fees and nobody else does? They have the gold…They make the rules.

Also in Oregon if you drive in an open range area and you hit a cow that has escaped through the fence not only do you not get compensated for the damage and injuries the cow caused but you have to pay the rancher for the cow as well. Why? The ranchers have they gold and they make the rules.

The taxpayers even buy greens mowers… Equipment used to mow golf course greens. This courtesy of the Agriculture department that, at the direction of the politicians, defines grass on golf courses as a "crop" making them eligible for taxpayer "crop" subsidies. How do they do this? They have the gold. They make the rules.

I could go on and on with examples of government designed to favor the ruling class at the expense of everybody else. Of course this isn't fair or just but this is how campaign contributions corrupt government. And this is how unlimited government works.

Chapter 7

Some of us are more equal than others

In George Orwell's Animal Farm he said: "All animals are equal but some animals are more equal than others."

When it comes to government while they claim we are all supposed to be equal under the law nothing could be further from the truth. They have even gone so far as to establish "protected classes" of people that are more privileged than others.

[A protected "class" is] …A group of people with a common characteristic who are legally protected from employment discrimination on the basis of that characteristic. Protected classes are created by both federal and state law.

Federal protected classes include:
Race.
Color.
Religion or creed.
National origin or ancestry.
Sex.
Age.
Physical or mental disability.
Veteran status.
Genetic information.
Citizenship…

So does this mean that some of us are unprotected? If so unprotected from what?

Also, we often assume that all regulations/rules/laws/taxes are applied and/or enforced equally. That's simply not the case. According to the institute of taxation and economic policy tax inequality index it is reported that in the state of Washington the poorest 20% pay almost 18% of what they make in taxes while the richest 1% pay only about 3% of what they make in taxes.

Imagine that. But it's nothing new because unlimited government is full of double standards that favor one group and penalize another. One example: Native Americans (Indians) on some reservations are exempted from sales, gasoline and other taxes. Again this is not a conspiracy theory with a few powerful people "behind the curtain" pulling this and that lever. This is simply what unlimited government is.

Chapter 8

The Government isn't here to help you

Aside from police and fire services that come when you call them (although whether and how public safety organizations respond to requests is subject to campaign contributions like most everything in government nowadays) and the military when it comes to national security the Government is not here to help us. The working class survives and often thrives in spite of government, not because of government.

In one sense we should not expect government to help us. With a few exceptions (like the truly disabled) people should "stand on their own two feet" and be contributors to society, not be continually feeding at the government trough.

Building permits are not to benefit the builder for safety or anything else. If the building inspector demands that certain things on the building and it is wrong and fails the "permitting" agencies are not liable. The owner is liable. Most of the time city sidewalks are owned by the city but maintained by the property owner. So if someone trips on a crack on the sidewalk and injures himself or herself the property owner is liable, not the city. The government isn't here to help you.

Aside from a small expense for recordkeeping the permit fees are nothing more than taxes. Also, when you apply for a building permit the county tax collector gets notified so they can "re-assess" your property which is "code" for raise your property taxes.

If one researches major fires or structural failures one will find that most had obvious code violations that were known for years prior to the disaster. The building code enforcement officials simply "looked the other way". It was reported that Pennsylvania Republican Governor Tom Ridge ordered that abortion clinics not be inspected by the state health department allowing Kermit Gosnell, perhaps the most prolific serial killer in our history, to continue his nefarious activities for some time.

A good case could be made to abolish most or all of those "Alphabet Soup" agencies. Most "regulatory" agencies are far more often lapdogs instead of watchdogs. A quick check of Federal, State and even local "regulatory" agencies will show that most of those who are appointed to run these agencies are executives in their respective industries.

For example: Insurance commissions most often are headed and staffed by insurance executives who are paid by the taxpayers as well as the companies they head up. Same for Agriculture, big pharmacy, transportation and virtually every other government agency we have.

Not only do these "regulatory" commissions not protect us they often actively work to screw us. Ever wonder why you get so many telemarketer calls when you have listed your name on the government do not call list? It's because the telemarketers are paying the politicians more than you are. You say: I'm paying them with my taxes. But the politicians don't see it that way. Remember the "higher order" where the campaign contributor rules. They could end problem telemarketing literally overnight but they don't because that would mean fewer campaign contributions or risking offending future potential campaign contributors.

Chapter 9

Secrecy = Tyranny

There is no constitutional right to privacy. If you think you have a right to privacy just tell the IRS that you won't report your financial transactions because they are "private" and see how far that gets you.

We now live in the "information age" where because of technology information is easily and inexpensively exchanged and disseminated. Ironically while we know more than we ever about the people around us (social media) and world events we know less about our government than we ever have.

A few years ago I was denied any information about a government sanctioned monopoly utility – which is public information - even though there is a clear statute allowing access to the information (Oregon Revised Statutes 62.440) and legal fees provided to enforce this provision.

But this same government sanctioned monopoly utility spent several thousand dollars to maintain a dossier on me which, when I was last allowed to see it, was about a 4 inch thick hard copy. Why do they do this? Because if they found something damning in my private life it could be used to "shut me up" or to retaliate by releasing this embarrassing information to the media.

So my "privacy" as a private citizen is a non-issue while public agencies have unlimited taxpayer money to pay lawyers to conceal and/ or defend public figures from even criminal behavior.

This privacy/secrecy issue is 180 degrees out of phase with the private citizen having near zero rights to privacy and public agencies invoking "privacy" when it comes to public money. When governments and the judiciary operate in "the light of day" they usually do the right thing. When allowed to operate in secret very little good happens.

For simply requesting public information I was fined $1,800.00 and threatened with jail time by Judge John Wolf, Wasco County (Oregon) circuit court. This happened a few months after my first wife died unexpectedly and they knew that. Judge Wolf was appointed by Oregon ex-governor John Kitzhaber who was forced out of office for selling influence shortly after Judge Wolf was appointed. The lawyer representing the state-sanctioned monopoly utility was paid $160,000.00 of our (ratepayer) money for about 20 hours work.

Why did this government sanctioned monopoly utility go to such great lengths and incur such a great cost (the ratepayers paid the bill, not the company officers) to make sure that they would not have to divulge any information? Probably because there was criminal activity and people would be going to jail if this was discovered. Similarly people who now request information from the Portland (Oregon) Public Schools get sued. Just what is it that they are trying to hide?

The best way to have limited government is to have open government. If any person or organization receives taxpayer money that person or organization should have taxpayer scrutiny. Of course there will be some national security issues that merit secrecy but they should be very few and well-defined.

Chapter 10

I owe my soul to the Government store

In 1890 Congress passed the Sherman Anti-trust act basically outlawing monopolistic business practices and providing triple damages for offenders. Since then the courts have held that monopoly interests are illegal unless they are established by the Government. Like the U.S. Postal service is a legal monopoly.

Today we have something just as bad and in some ways worse than the conditions that drove the Sherman Anti-Trust act: The de-facto monopoly established by campaign contributions

Just about everything that the Government sells us whether that be water, sewer, electric power, garbage disposal, credit, health care, housing, etcetera costs far more than the actual cost of delivering the product or service and much of the money collected from us (the "profits") get "kicked back" to various private individuals with "vested" interests. "Vested" means campaign contribution investments.

Our government Sanctioned monopoly power company here outside of The Dalles, Oregon, Wasco Electric Co-operative, has had double-digit rate increases every year for over 10 years. Much of that money goes to a very wealthy Portland lawyer because they give money to the politicians to make that happen. This happens in spite of the fact that it is illegal for monopoly utilities to give money directly to the politicians. So they give the money (our money for their benefit) indirectly through lobbyists.

Our power rates have gone up so much over the years that many people have trouble paying their power bill. So how do they deal with that? Wasco Electric started a WE Care program. Meaning: Wasco Electric Cares. The Scheme: People can donate tax deductible amounts to a fund which gets distributed to those who Wasco Electric deems "needy". There is no definition of "needy" here so conceivably this money could go to very wealthy individuals.

You can apply for assistance in paying your electric bill but you must qualify. How do you qualify? You kiss their feet. How nice of them! Jack up the power rates so high that the average person has trouble paying their power bill and then accept donations so some wealthy folks can pay less in taxes.

Same goes with selling us healthcare. We have by far the world's most expensive healthcare but only rank near the "middle of the pack" when it comes to overall health as a nation relative to the rest of the world. In fact the average life expectancy is going down, not up. Why? Because the price of health care is going up the quality of health care is going down. If you could increase the sales and price of any product while reducing the quality - what it costs you to deliver that product or service – that means what you make from each transactions – the profits – go up. And that's what we have with healthcare thanks in large part to campaign contributions.

A number of politicians over the years have expressed concerns over the number of "uninsured" Americans. But just because you buy insurance doesn't mean it covers what you need it to cover. Often, because our government limits choices (the monopoly aspect of all of this) insurance companies in effect force you to buy unneeded services you will never use in order to even get insurance. Like pregnancy coverage for an elderly couple.

Also politicians often trumpet the fact that they "made" insurance companies cover pre-existing conditions. But what they don't tell you is that coverage for pre-existing conditions costs far more than regular health insurance. The insurance companies are happy to provide the high cost pre-existing condition coverage but many people simply cannot afford that. More correctly the insurance companies "made" the politicians (via campaign contributions) mandate coverage for pre-existing conditions because they make more money on that.

Health care sold by the government is not to benefit the sick but to benefit the health care providers who "pony up" huge campaign contributions to make this happen. The byzantine health care system is not designed to give us something but to get something out of us. Often employers sell us healthcare on the premise that group policies cost less and the net more in the way of services. But what if the employer profits from the health care they sell they sell their employees? There's nothing in the law that says they can't charge the employee, say, $200.00 per month for their healthcare when the employer pays $50.00 per month for that healthcare and the employers keep the difference.

And why do we need to give out our social security number and tell the healthcare company what we make in order to get heath care? Do you buy anything else that way? Imagine going to the tire store to buy tires for your car. The tire salesperson says something like: "Before we can sell you some tires we need to have your social security number and see your most recent tax returns". Upon hearing this most people would immediately head for the next tire store.

We won't let the tire store do that to us but we will let the health care providers do that to us using the government as a "front". It's really the health care providers driving all of this again via campaign contributions but the information they get from you for free (social security number and income/financial information via your tax returns) is very valuable and can be sold, shared or traded on many levels. You say there are laws in place that prevent that? Name one.

Not only that but there are software programs that organize and analyze your information to determine how much you are able to pay as well as how much you are willing to pay for various health care services. This along with your health history (buying habits) all determines what they charge you for a certain medical procedure. Imagine if you were a car salesman and had instant access to your customers' income and car buying habits. That would give you a tremendous advantage. You could adjust your pricing to exploit your customer to the max. And that's exactly what's happening with health care thanks to massive campaign contributions.

Also, why do the health care companies tell us what they paid for something? When the insurance company tells you they paid $6,000.00 to a certain hospital for your hernia operation how do you know they actually paid that? There is no law that says that those figures must be true and correct. If you walked into the insurance company office and asked to see a copy of the invoice they paid for your hernia operation you would be told to take a long walk on a short pier. It's an unwritten rule in business is that you never tell anybody (except the IRS) what you pay for anything. So why do health care companies tell us what they paid for your health care services?

Does congressman Blowhard want to you or a loved one suffer physical pain or financial insolvency because of an unexpected disease or injury? Of course not. But if that happens congressman Blowhard doesn't care because there is this "higher order" where the campaign contributors get what they want and the "little people" working class suffers the consequences.

All of this brought to you by unlimited government.

Chapter 11

It's not who votes…It's who counts the votes

There are several voting systems available now that will insure a nearly 100% accurate vote count. And that's exactly why they are not widely used.

I spent 10 years spending my own time and money running for election to public office only to find out that the elections were rigged. I ran for a seat on the board of Wasco Electric Co-operative, a state sanctioned monopoly electric power utility that is supposed to be "owned" by the ratepayers who buy power from them and is supposed to have government oversight.

The elections are rigged because the law governing Oregon Co-operatives allows them to be rigged. No, the law does not spell out that Oregon Co-operatives are allowed to "rig" elections. It's what is *not* in the law that's the problem, not what is in the law. The law (Oregon revised statutes 62) requires that board of director elections be held. But the law does not require these elections to be fair and impartial.

The net result is that the Co-operative counts their own votes, installs whomever they want regardless of the vote tally. Basically they can throw all of the votes in the shredder and install whomever they want and it is all legal. The votes all go to a board member who can "purge" "problem" votes if he/she deems necessary because they know who voted. It is not a secret ballot.

The state of Oregon has vote by mail which makes it easier to "rig" or "swing" elections. One could make that case that if one doesn't care enough about good government to make a trip to their local polling place once every two years or so then they don't deserve good government. One more time that's what unlimited government is and it takes constant vigilance to make sure that government stays limited.

Chapter 12

Our representatives aren't supposed to work together

Our founding fathers knew this well. The "balance of power" between the executive (president) the legislature (the congress) and the judiciary (the courts) was done purposely to "hamstring" government. They knew if government was given a "blank check" that they would "do it" to the people instead of for the people.

If we wanted a government that "got things done we should just elect a King or Queen and give him or her absolute power. The problem is that when a ruler has absolute power the people are powerless to stop him or her short of a bloody revolution. It is true that absolute power corrupts absolutely.

Often the media will exhort the legislature to "work together" or "work across the aisle" with the template being that everything that comes out of government is good. Unfortunately much of the time that isn't the case. When I was running for Oregon State Representative during the only candidate forum the incumbent would agree to appear at the local media moderator asked something like: What would you do to help government work together to 'get things done'. I replied that if it's bad legislation I would hope that they don't work together.

The reason our founding fathers organized government as they did is because too much power concentrated in the hands of too few individuals resulted in tyranny. The "balance of powers" with the separate executive (president), legislative (congress) and judicial (courts) branches was designed to slow government down in order to insure that whatever came out of government was well vetted and satisfactory to the majority.

Often governments and private interests form "public-private" partnerships which are typically nothing more than one more pipeline for taxpayer money to flow to the private party…Again made possible by campaign contributions. The government should not fund or hold any stake in any private enterprise.

Many states have provisions precluding government involvement in private ventures most of which are ignored or not enforced. The Oregon State constitution contains one such proviso. Below is the text of the Oregon State Constitution section 6 along with comments by law professor Jack Bogdanski (from Jack Bog's Blog) illustrating the problems with government involvement in private industries.

Section 6. State not to be stockholder in company; exceptions. (1) The state shall not subscribe to, or be interested in the stock of any company, association or corporation. However, as provided by law the state may hold and dispose of stock, including stock already received, that is donated or bequeathed; and may invest, in the stock of any company, association or corporation, any funds or moneys that:

(a) Are donated or bequeathed for higher education purposes;

(b) Are the proceeds from the disposition of stock that is donated or bequeathed for higher education purposes, including stock already received; or

(c) Are dividends paid with respect to stock that is donated or bequeathed for higher education purposes, including stock already received.

(2) Notwithstanding the limits contained in subsection (1) of this section, the state may hold and dispose of stock:

(a) Received in exchange for technology created in whole or in part by a public institution of post-secondary education; or

(b) Received prior to December 5, 2002, as a state asset invested in the creation or development of technology or resources within Oregon. [Constitution of 1859; Amendment proposed by H.J.R. 11, 1955, and adopted by the people Nov. 6, 1956; Amendment proposed by H.J.R. 27, 1969, and adopted by the people Nov. 3, 1970; Amendment proposed by S.J.R. 17, 2001, and adopted by the people May 21, 2002]

Section 9. Limitations on powers of county or city to assist corporations. No county, city, town or other municipal corporation, by vote of its citizens, or otherwise, shall become a stockholder in any joint company, corporation or association, whatever, or raise money for, or loan its credit to, or in aid of, any such company, corporation or association. Provided, that any municipal corporation designated as a port under any general or special law of the state of Oregon, may be empowered by statute to raise money and expend the same in the form of a bonus to aid in establishing water transportation lines between such port and any other domestic or foreign port or ports, and to aid in establishing water transportation lines on the interior rivers of this state, or on the rivers between Washington and Oregon, or on the rivers of Washington and Idaho reached by navigation from Oregon's rivers; any debts of a municipality to raise money created for the aforesaid purpose shall be incurred only on approval of a majority of those voting on the question, and shall not, either singly or in the aggregate, with previous debts and liabilities incurred for that purpose, exceed one per cent of the assessed valuation of all property in the municipality. [Constitution of 1859; Amendment proposed by S.J.R. 13, 1917, and adopted by the people June 4, 1917]

[Jack Bogdanski's comments]

Fast and loose with the state constitution

Article XI, section 6 of the Oregon Constitution states in part: "The state shall not subscribe to, or be interested in the stock of any company, association or corporation."

But here's a story about the state making a huge loan to a startup company. Now, the tax lawyer in me knows that at some point, a so-called loan to a high-risk venture is more properly classified as equity rather than debt. In other words, as an economic matter it's a preferred stock, rather than a loan, because there's substantial risk that it might not be repaid. That's especially true if it's subordinated, expressly or implicitly, to other debts that the borrower owes.

Has that theory got any legs when it comes to the Oregon constitutional prohibition? And if so, on which side of the debt-equity line does this "loan" fall?

Then there's this slick maneuver here in Portland:

State rules prevent the city from investing directly in private companies. So the city considered lending the money instead.

Now, though, the PDC has decided to grant the money to a new, self-perpetuating not-for-profit organization.

That five-member group will hire an investment manager to handle the city's money and solicit private investment to augment the city's stake.

The "state rules" that the O reporter is talking about are presumably Article XI, section 9 of the Oregon constitution, which reads in part:

No county, city, town or other municipal corporation, by vote of its citizens, or otherwise, shall become a stockholder in any joint company, corporation or association, whatever, or raise money for, or loan its credit to, or in aid of, any such company, corporation or association.

Is that constitutional provision as easy to get around as the PDC is making it out to be? You just set up a nonprofit and launder the stock investment -- "the city's stake" -- through that group? Is the constitution that flimsy?

I know, I know -- this is Portland. I shouldn't even bother to ask.

Just one more example of unlimited government in action.

Chapter 13

Very little happens in a Vacuum

Often those of us in the working class are told by those of the government/ ruling class that something "just happened" and most of the time that isn't true. In almost every case there is a reason something happens. Just because we don't see or understand the reason doesn't mean there isn't one. Very little happens in a vacuum.

Politicians often cite their ability to "cut through the red tape" of government bureaucracy but if government ran efficiently and competently we wouldn't need the politicians to "cut through the red tape". The politicians created the byzantine government and then we are supposed to praise them for "cutting the red tape" when they are the ones who created the red tape to begin with.

There is a troubling trend of having lawyers present at every government agency board meeting. This is problematic on several fronts. Are these agencies incompetent or corrupt that they have to constantly be worried about being sued? As for me personally I make a point to conduct all of my affairs honestly and above-board so I won't get sued. Sure, it happens to the best of us but I don't need a lawyer to watch my every move.

Most everybody knows or can cite instances where that people say or don't say certain things just when a lawyer is present. It alters the meeting discourse which often isn't a good thing. Lawyers should never be allowed to attend board meetings. But they do because agency business cannot be conducted lawfully outside of a board meeting. So the lawyer's "being there" can prevent the board from doing stupid (as far as the lawyer is concerned) things like firing him or retaining another lawyer.

There's nothing wrong government agencies retaining legal counsel. However the ethical way to do this is if there is a legal issue that comes up then the board should direct the superintendent or head administrator contact the lawyer after the meeting to obtain legal advice about a certain issue and then report on what the lawyer said at the next board meeting.

Remember that the lawyer is at the board meeting first and foremost to advance his interests, not the interests of the agency or the citizens they are supposed to represent. If that means suing someone or advising the board to do something stupid that gets the government agency sued that's more money for the lawyer. There's also the threat of individual board members getting sued if they say or do something the lawyer doesn't like. There's nothing in the law that says that can't happen.

Have you ever wondered why bureaucrats are so dumb? It's because the lawyers don't want anybody that's too bright in those positions. Neither do they want the village idiot because that can be embarrassing but they don't want anybody too bright either. But the lawyers actually want to be sued because it means more money for them and if some bureaucrat says or does something stupid that triggers a lawsuit…All the better.

A few years ago there was a big push to have universal daycare. But we already have universal daycare. It's called public schools. Most public schools nowadays do very little in the way of education but much in the way of indoctrination. For a while I volunteered to teach electronics at a nearby public school. The classes were very popular with the students and taught a useful skill that they could use any time in their lives anywhere in the world.

One would think those credentials would be well received and I would be offered a contract to continue this educational endeavor. Wrong. Public schools are nothing more than job mills for teachers and administrators. The administrator has a slot he has to fill with a union member teacher and that's all that happens.

That's how we get wood shop teachers teaching robotics…A subject most wood shop teachers normally know very little about. So the school district spends a lot of money and cheats the kids out of any sort of education in this subject because they have a mandate to fill the slot, not educate the children.

Public schools are very much political animals. I found this out when I went to work for a public school district some years ago. I worked about 18 months only to be forced out and my job given to a political crony. This school district was so brazen about this that I even knew who was going to replace me.

What about union representation that I had paid dues to that entire time? They were worthless. And the school district knew they were worthless. That's why they were our union. While there are many laws that compel you to pay union dues…They are taken out of your paycheck like taxes and if you don't pay them you get fired. There is nothing in the law that says that the union has to do anything for you. You cannot sue them for malpractice, theft of services or anything else if they refuse to represent you diligently.

I worked at The Home Depot for 9 years and I can tell you that Home Depot management is terrified about union organization. And for good reason: An effective union presence could literally shut them down. But given the current state of union representation they don't have much to worry about. Most employees know that and correctly reason that they might as well keep the money that would normally go to paying union dues and take their chances with management.

Catholic priest abuse has been going on for millennia (thousands of years). The pope could end this abuse problem literally overnight but he won't because if he took any meaningful action he wouldn't be pope anymore. It's just what they are. The lawyers have figured out how to tap the great wealth the Catholic system by suing them periodically. If you look closely there is nothing in these "settlements" that ends the abuses. The sexual abuses can go on as long as some money is given to the lawyers from time to time.

Ever wonder why there are so many "loopholes" in the laws? Most of them don't end up there by accident. "Loopholes" can be implemented by adding language to the law or deliberately leaving out language that should be in the law. There are few "unintended consequences" to laws and policies as Rush likes to say. The politicians know full well what the consequences of their actions are but *they don't care!* Remember the "higher order" where the campaign contributor is KING.

Abortion and Euthanasia are nothing more than the power to determine who lives and who dies and the money that goes along with that power. If you will examine the laws dealing with these activities you will find that there is little or no language in the law to prevent abuses that inevitably goes along with these practices. That's by design and not an accident.

If Grandma, who happens to have a sizable estate signs over that estate to an acquaintance while impaired by chemotherapy drugs before being "euthanized" what are the true beneficiaries to do? Sure, the beneficiaries can sue but whoever first gets control over the estate has unlimited estate money to buy lawyers to defend even criminal activity. It's likely the true beneficiaries will get the estate money back Minus the money that went to the interloper's lawyer as well as the beneficiaries' lawyer.

That could be very little money when it's all over with. But since the lawyers are big campaign contributors we have the laws we have. What's the solution for this? The estate trustee should use his/her own money to defend a legal challenge by the beneficiaries which could be refunded should the challenge be determined to be without merit. But that would result in less legal costs which is why we have what we have.

Every few years the media will run articles decrying the existence of offshore bank accounts as a way for the ruling class to escape paying taxes. Congress could end offshore bank accounts literally overnight if they wanted to. But they don't want to. Remember the ruling class makes campaign contributions and that's why they are the ruling class.

It has been reported that the U.S. immigration laws not only fail to discourage child trafficking but actually encourage it. How? Thousands of requests by men to bring in child and adolescent brides to live in the United States were approved over the past decade and this is legal because there are no minimum age requirements. This not an oversight or unintended legislative "slip-up". This was done purposely to allow that kind of activity. Of course public outrage may effect a change in the law but that doesn't help the thousands of young victims who have already had requests approved.

Have you ever wondered why high-ranking government and some private company officials end up with huge retirement packages? Like the former president of Michigan State University who was implicated in the Larry Nasser abuse cover-up to name one. It's called "hush money". Most of these "deals" are revocable all or in part for specified or unspecified "breaches". Translated this means if the official exposes wrongdoing by the organization or some similar "lack of fidelity" his or her retirement money can be in jeopardy. That is very effective in allowing these abuses to go undetected for years.

Who really benefits from our massive social programs? The poor or the rich? The answer is both. The working poor get subsistence living for free and the rich get substantially reduced labor costs. Many of us could do quite well working at minimum wage if we had our basic needs of food, housing, utilities, education, medical care, etc. paid by someone else…In this case the working class via taxation of the working class in large part. This scheme also has the overall effect of depressing wages in other areas.

One could not honestly call illegal immigrants flocking to this country to serve the ruling class demand for cheap labor as "human slavery" because they are coming here voluntarily. But it could be viewed as "economic slavery" similar to indentured servitude. The threat of deportation gives the "slaveowner" a "club" to hold over the head of the illegal immigrant so they will be more tolerant of the low wages and poor working conditions they must deal with to live in this country.

In many ways having a huge influx of cheap labor illegal immigrants is better for the ruling class than the classic slavery business model we knew before the civil war. Whereas the classic slaveowner had to provide the basic food, clothing, housing and medical needs of the slaves today the working class taxpayers provide the basic food, clothing, housing and medical needs for the "slaves".

Ever wonder why the U.S. is constantly involved in endless wars all over the world that have no defined victory or exit strategy? Basically these wars function to "use up" military equipment so that the suppliers can sell the military replacement parts. Unfortunately these wars also "used up" our men and women in uniform but we can't replace them. This is called the military-industrial complex. In 1961 former president Dwight Eisenhower warned us of this phenomenon and the consequences of such policies.

Not that long ago if we had a war everybody went to war. That included the sons and daughters of the very wealthy. Elvis Presley served in the military. Former president John F. Kennedy served in the military. These and many others were for very wealthy families who could have spent their time elsewhere but when their country called they were there.

With the Vietnam war all of that changed. People grew weary of seven years of watching their family and friends come back in body bags with no defined victory or exit strategy. All of this went on while the children of the wealthy dodged the draft with "deferments" which were nothing more than exemptions from military service.

Congress responded by increasing the pay and benefits for service members and creating an all-volunteer military. Now our men and women in uniform still get sent to fight wars that have no defined victory or exit strategy but they get paid better and don't have to enlist if they don't want to. This is also why these wars are staged in far-off countries because Americans would never tolerate military action on their soil.

Does congressman Blowhard lay awake nights plotting how to kill your son or daughter in a war zone? Of course not. But if your son or daughter does get killed in a war that has no logical or strategic importance to our country congressman Blowhard *doesn't care*. Congressman Blowhard has a "higher order" and that is to obtain and increase the number and value of campaign contributions and if part of this includes the death of your son or daughter in military service that's just too bad.

Indeed very little does happen in a vacuum.

Chapter 14

Law and disorder

The power (and money) to sue is the power to destroy. Often lawsuits are filed without any intention of winning. The objective is to waste your time and money. It's nothing more than legalized extortion. With "hit and run" lawsuits the plaintiff's lawyer sues you and makes several demands. After spending much time and money preparing your defense the plaintiff drops the lawsuit. This should constitute abuse of process and you should be able to recover the money you spent to defend yourself to that point. Not so. If this were the case there would be far fewer lawsuits filed which is exactly why we don't have that proviso.

One could say that the money to defend against lawsuits is a de-facto "get out of jail free" card. Governments almost without exception have the power to use public money to defend those in government from even criminal activity. They also have the power to use public money to pay for sexual harassment settlements and the substantial legal fees that invariably result from these "settlements" in most cases.

The first thing my lawyer asked me when we requested public information which required a lawsuit is "what do you know about the Judge?" The fact one even needs to ask that is a sad commentary on our judicial system. In this case neither one of us knew much about the judge as he was a relatively new appointee at the time.

When we went forward with the litigation it became obvious that this judge wasn't the least bit impartial. He could have dismissed the lawsuit and ended our attempt to enforce government transparency in accordance with the law. But the opposing lawyer wouldn't have as much money that way. So he fined me $1,800.00 and threatening me with jail time even though the state statute we asserted (Oregon Revised Statutes 62.440) provided legal fees to enforce (not defend against) this action.

Judges in most states have "judicial review" councils or something similar set up ostensibly to deal with bad judges. However, to remove a judge, most specify that a pattern of abuses must be evident before any action can be taken to remove a judge. Do we need a "pattern" of unethical, illegal or dishonest behavior to take action against anyone else when it comes to obeying the law?

Do we need a "pattern" of car thefts before the police can arrest a car theft suspect? Usually only one car theft will get the average person arrested and charged. Does the IRS need a "pattern" of tax law violations before they can "go after" the taxpayer? No. Everywhere else one violation is more than enough. Except for judges. And if anybody should have higher standard with all of the power they have it's a judge.

In fact there was a judge in Michigan that openly demanded sex from some females that came before his court in exchange for a favorable ruling. While the Michigan state legislature took steps to sanction this judge but did not impeach and remove him as provided by the state constitution which the lawmakers pledged (swore in the oath of office) to uphold. Why? Because corrupt lawmakers need corrupt judges to get what they want.

Some laws are written with the lawmakers knowing full well that the law cannot be enforced in court. They're there to try and demonstrate to the voters that they are "doing something" for the people when in fact it's only "window dressing". Like reducing the speed limit from 25 miles per hour to 20 miles per hour in school zones. Yup, that's really going to make a difference but the lawmakers can say that they "did something" for school safety.

Some laws are written so that they are very difficult and/or expensive to enforce. This along with the sheer volume of lawsuits filed and two or three years before the lawsuit even received a hearing in court often discourages people from seeking justice in our court system even though they know they have a good case and would probably win.

Then if you sue the government not only are you going up against someone who can use the long delays to continue doing the activity that got them sued in the first place but they have unlimited taxpayer money to defend even criminal activity.

That's what we get with unlimited government.

Chapter 15

Our values Ourselves

Values are what divide and define people. Not race. Not religion. Not national origin. Values are what we deem to be important. That doesn't mean that everybody practices these values all of the time. It means that there is an overall respect for these values and being regarded as the right and proper way to live one's life. In other words, it's the right thing to do.

I eat right, get adequate sleep and watch my weight not because I'm afraid I'm going to die prematurely if I don't. I do it because it's the right thing to do. Same goes for staying faithful to my wife, paying my bills and taxes and "giving back" to the community as well as other positive endeavors. Also don't take anything without paying for it and clean up your messes. This could be called "integrity" or "honor" and it is the main focus of what we call "Judeo-Christian" values.

I question those who would demand things like school lunches for their children. I would be insulted if someone stated or implied that I could not or would not adequately care for my children. I simply wouldn't allow my children go hungry. Even the most rotten parents wouldn't let it happen. If I was dying of some horrible disease and could not function normally that's one thing. But most of the time that's not the case.

I don't have any debt for the same reason and when I have to use credit I use it sparingly and pay it off as quickly as I can. I'm not afraid of going bankrupt. It's just the right thing to do. If I were dying of cancer or other terrible disease and couldn't pay my bills no reasonable person would have a problem "writing this off" their books. Just because it is possible and legal to "settle" your debt doesn't mean it's ethical or the right thing to do.

Unfortunately we have a large number of residents in this country that do not share those values. Limited government does not work without a strong Judeo-Christian value base. People that feel they are "entitled" to other people's money and do not value or understand why we have limited government. In a nutshell we should value limited government because unlimited government is tyranny. Unlimited government is great for those who are in government but miserable for the rest of us.

My great-grandfather emigrated from Germany over 100 years ago. My Grandfather grew up in a German settlement in Minnesota. For years I thought he was ashamed to be German because of what happened during World War II and related events because he never talked much about his German heritage.

It was only some years later that I realized the he really wasn't ashamed of his German heritage. He wasn't German any more. He was American and that's what he wanted to be. The German language and culture, while not bad in any way, was just a distant memory and he was into bigger and better things in America.

Demonstrations like refusing to stand for the National Anthem at sports events: Standing for the National Anthem does not mean that you agree with everything America is or does or that America is perfect and has never done anything wrong. Standing for the National Anthem is simply a show of respect. Respect for the land you happen to be residing in at the time. You don't have to "love it" but if it's a problem to you then leave.

If you like Mexico or any other utopia you escaped from so much then why don't you move back there? If our country is so unjust and oppressive then go back to wherever you came from.

Author and film critic Michael Medved once said: "One can take the individual out of the Ghetto but you can't take the Ghetto out of the individual". What does that mean? That's values and culture. If someone is not bothered by trash, graffiti and broken windows everywhere that's an intrinsic value that they are expressing.

Many of us would try to at least clean up and repair our surroundings as best we could rather than stand or sit on street corners and watch the world go by. That's also the expression of our values. Values emanate from within outward, not from the outside environment inward. Our "environment", while it colors our world view, does not establish our values.

The Bible affirms that fact in many places one of them being Matthew chapter 15.

[Verse 17] "Don't you see that whatever enters the mouth goes into the stomach and then out of the body? 18] But the things that come out of a person's mouth come from the heart, and these defile them. 19] For out of the heart come evil thoughts—murder, adultery, sexual immorality, theft, false testimony, slander. 20] These are what defile a person; but eating with unwashed hands does not defile them."

Evil actions are not "triggered" by the environment a person lives in. Evil actions start with evil inside coming out. Example: People commit suicide not because problems outside of them. They commit suicide because of problems inside of them being manifested in their actions.

Our founding fathers understood the nature of man from biblical teaching and long-term observation and wisely crafted a limited government that would work to benefit the average citizen. Unlimited government does just the opposite by bestowing privilege to the ruling class at the expense of the average citizens.

Chapter 16

USA Toady

Why do governments purchase advertising? You know…Those public service ads that tell us things like don't drink and drive, don't text and drive, use your seat belts, etc. We all see and hear dozens of them every day. Taxpayer money makes sure that media outlets report certain things.

However, far more important and useful to our government masters is that purchasing advertising makes sure that media outlets don't report certain things. How many newspapers and radio and television stations report bad things about their paying advertisers? And why do Rush, Lars and Hannity accept government advertising?

All media outlets have unused "air" or (in the case of print and internet newspapers) "space" that cannot be sold for advertising for a variety of reasons. Some advertising is seasonal with more coming during certain times like the holiday seasons and less at other times. What better way to "sell" this space than to sell it to the government.

There are a lot of advantages for the media outlet here.

- It fills space that the media outlet would have difficulty filling with other content.
- They can sell this space at "discount" rates to the government and the government doesn't care when or how often these ads run. Only that they run.

- This is a win-win for the media outlets and the government. Media outlets get money in exchange for not reporting certain things which casts governments in a bad light even if it's true.

To give you an idea of just how bad the media is when I ran for state representative all of the candidates received notice that the Bend Bulletin, the local paper serving Bend, Oregon, announced that they were having a candidate's forum and that all of the candidates for that particular election were invited. Not wanting to miss out on an opportunity I attended and found all of the other candidates, some of whom had traveled great distances to be there, but none of the incumbents were there. Aside from the challengers the only people that were at the event were the Bend Bulletin advertising representatives who were eager to sell us advertising. Talk about Bait and Switch.

With the media "in bed" with government and partially funded by them we get more and more unlimited government. Not a good thing.